HAIR IN FUNNY PLACES

Babette Cole

A TOM MASCHLER BOOK

JONATHAN CAPE

LONDON

Ted, when will I grow up to be a 'grown up'?

That depends on Mr and Mrs Hormone.
They are in charge of growing up.

They live inside you and are so tiny
that you can't see them.

If you could this is what you would see.

When your mum was little
she was just like you.

And for about eleven years Mr and Mrs Hormone slept peacefully inside her, until her body clock woke them up! This made them very grumpy!

Brrrr !

It was time to mix the potions that turn children
into adults and send them round her body.

Mrs Hormone's mixtures
began to work and
your mum sprouted
small bosoms

and hair
in funny places ...

her voice deepened.

Then she found a tiny
drop of blood in her
knickers!

It meant one day
she could be your
mummy.

A year or two
later the bleeding
happened
once a month.

Sometimes
it made her
feel awful.

But she was pleased
to be growing tall.

The potion made her mad about boys.

At the same time
it gave her spots!

She worried in case
she wasn't developing
in the same way as
her friends.
But Mrs Hormone's
mixtures do not
affect everyone at
the same time.

The stuff made her feel
very up and down;
some days she felt
pleased with
herself

AAAgh!

but on others she was angry with everyone.

Never mind.
She had a grown up body
which she liked.

So did the boys!

Now let me tell you about your dad. When the Hormones got to work on him he was only about eight and looked very like a girl - except for his small penis.

To make him grow up they worked out
a whole new chemical mixture.

They flooded his
insides with it!

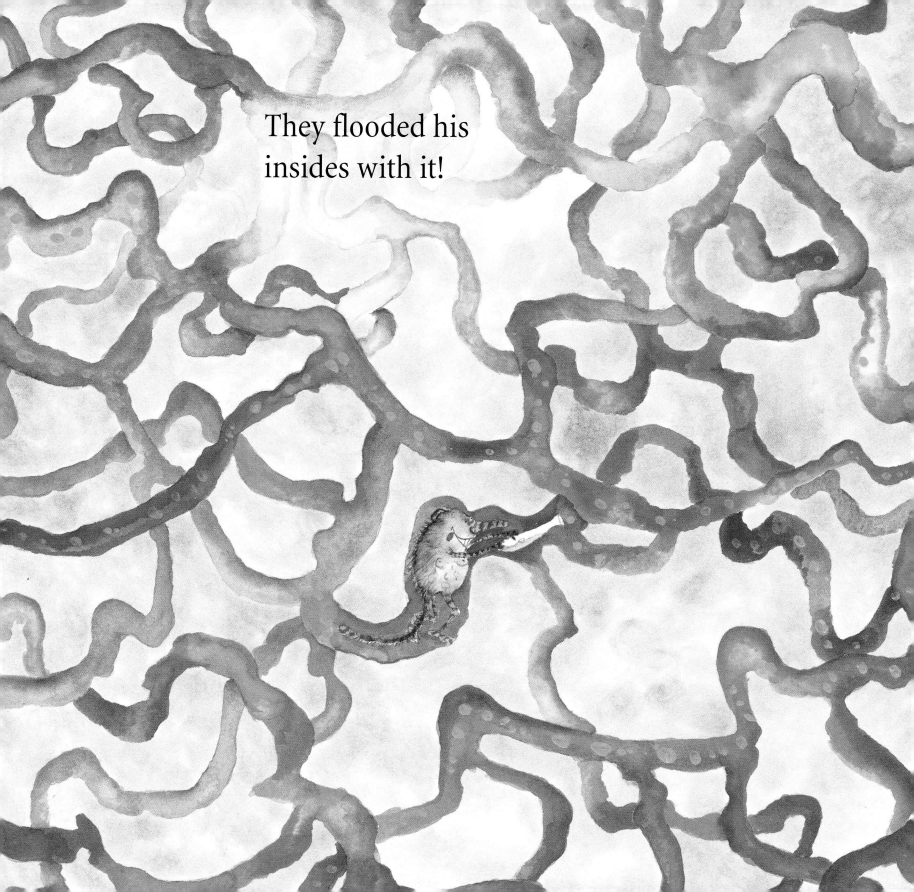

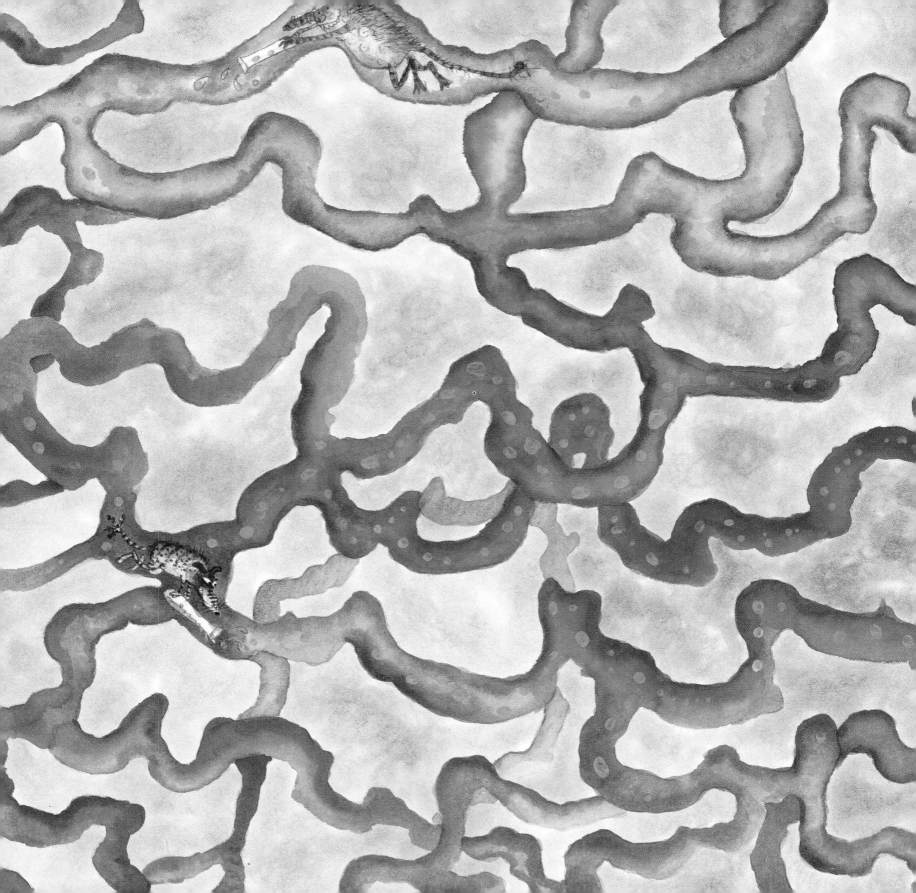

A year or two later
his shoulders
broadened
and his penis
thickened.

He too grew hair
in funny places.

As for his voice,
it was deep one
minute and
squeaky the next.

He soon began
to take an
interest
in girls.

Inside his penis,
Mr Hormone was
lurking with another
dollop of the mixture.

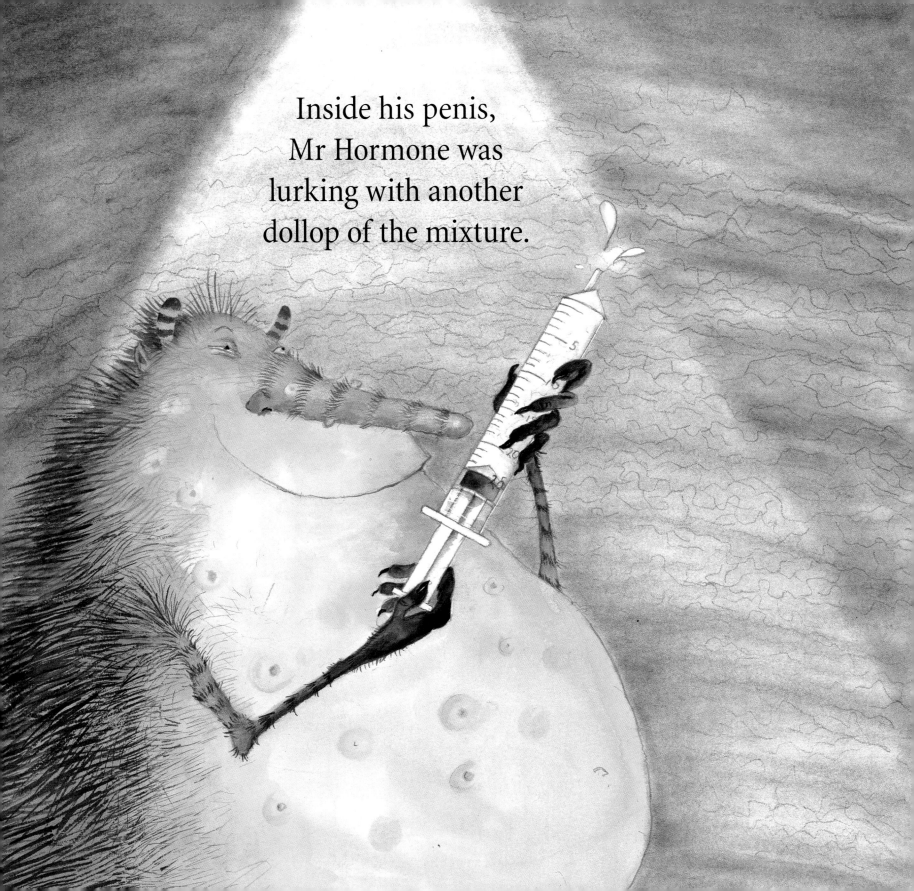

This made it grow big and small whenever it wanted.
Then some sticky stuff actually came out.
It meant one day he could be your dad!

He wanted to kiss girls but the Hormones
had made him spotty and smelly.

By the time he was eighteen the spots had disappeared and he was a handsome young man.

Then Mr and Mrs Hormone's dog invented the wildest potion of all.

When your mum and dad met
the potion was sent whizzing round their bodies.

They went crazy
about one another!

And they made you.

I suppose when you grow up,
you won't want me any more.

Oh no, Ted, you are so wise
I will always love you.